Ordinary Hours

Ordinary Hours · **Karen Enns**

BRICK BOOKS

BRICK BOOKS · 431 BOLER ROAD, BOX 20081
LONDON, ONTARIO N6K 4G6 · WWW.BRICKBOOKS.CA

Cover image: William Henry Fox Talbot, *Leaves of Orchidea*, 1839,
J. Paul Getty Museum, Los Angeles.
The author photo was taken by Barb McDougall.

This book is set in Williams Caslon, designed by William Berkson
in 2009 and published by Font Bureau.
Design and layout by Cheryl Dipede.

Copyright © Karen Enns 2014.

Library and Archives Canada Cataloguing in Publication
Enns, Karen, 1960-, author
    Ordinary hours / Karen Enns.
ISBN 978-1-926829-90-6 (pbk.)
    I. Title.
PS8609.N66O73 2014   C811'.6   C2013-907371-X

We acknowledge the Canada Council for the Arts, and the Ontario
Arts Council for their support of our publishing program.

Contents

I

Prelude..........5
A Sign..........6
Storm..........7
Bare Life..........8
There Are Words Carved in Wood..........9
Muse..........10
Better Days..........11
The Rooster..........12
Townline..........13
A Gull Will Almost Land..........14
Pianists at Night..........15
Dust and Salt..........16
Passing By..........17
La cathédrale engloutie..........18
Open Bloom..........19

II

After..........23
Getting the Chimney Repaired..........24
Third Floor, Queenston Street Wing..........25
Tulips..........26
At First..........27
Stamina..........28
William Street Elegies..........29
Yellow Chair..........33
At the Bus Stop..........34
Eva..........35
Soup..........36
To Adam Zagajewski..........37
Sotto Voce..........38
The Hired Man..........39
Cicadas..........40
Violets..........42

III

Premonition..........45
What I Was Told to Do with My Soul..........46

Temptation..........48
November..........49
Suite for Tools..........50
Devotion..........53
The Crow..........54
In the Waiting Room..........55
Sisters..........56
Underground..........57
The Nail..........58
To Walk into That Beauty..........59
The Polish Class Sits Down to Dinner..........60
Metaphor..........61
Restraint..........62
Now..........63
Wonder..........65
Winter..........66

Acknowledgements..........69
About the Author..........71

for my parents
Amalie and Peter
with love

I

Prelude

Nothing is happening.
Rachmaninoff plays in the other room
but there is nothing here. No heavy veils lifting,
no burning cities or collapsing kingdoms.
No one is drinking wine and talking politics.
No one is laughing uproariously in their chairs.
There are no communists in sight, high priests
or seers, prophets or angels, no dark horses
taking to the hills. Not a train in view
or bicycle, no bells or chimes,
the light is simply window light.
There is no moon, no path
to take you through the underbrush,
through rain or sleet to clearings and wide vistas
or a glimpse of lemon trees against a low stone wall.
No one comes carrying a package,
an orphaned child or green apples in their arms.
There are no hands at the window, no doves
or nightingales perched on the eaves,
no blooming trellises or dusted flagstone walks.
There are no tin roofs from which to see
the domes of cathedrals or the sea.
No rivers, nomads or sacred bulls.
The walls are white.
The floor is made of wood.
There is absence, not emptiness,
and something close to echo.

A Sign

In June we were carried away by the length of days.
We walked the streets like lovers, full of the light
and the whole green, blooming world.
We imagined ourselves eternal.
And when the cottonwoods released their white down
over the fields and the schoolyard square,
the children playing
lifted their hands and faces to the sky
like shepherds toward a star.
In disbelief it seemed at the time,
but when I think of it now,
believing.

Storm

Always the aunts with their thick legs
and the straining lawn chairs under the chestnut trees.
That Sunday then, a wind kicked in,
the chestnuts over us were huge and swaying
and the first drops of rain came hard.
The aunts began with warnings
as they gathered up the plates and cups,
the chicken salad, plums, calling
as we ducked and ran and shimmied under bushes
in that strange press of air.
They called again.
Again we laughed and hid,
and then they drew out long and razor-sharp,
the story of a day much the same, a gathering
exactly so, and a storm that came up from the lake
as sudden as sin. Main branches snapped,
the barn door blew wide open with a crack of light,
a white cut slicing through the sky.
A day the lightning chose a boy about my size,
who wasn't listening,
standing underneath a tree,
who wouldn't come when he was called
and next thing anybody knew,
he'd disappeared, his shoes
the only thing he'd left behind,
small, open mouths
where his feet had been,
the laces split clean through.

Bare Life

Is the woman sitting on a bench shelling peas.

Is the wood-frame house behind her
and a line of poplars to the east
and then the shed.

Is the question of wind.

Is her eye fixed on the camera's eye
with something like refusal.

Is knowing that a stone thrown into water
has its moment of pure sound.

Is wholeness. Claim.

There Are Words Carved in Wood

There are words carved in wood, on tree trunks, doors and windowsills.

There is silence as enormous, unframed thought, thought as unframed silence.
Huge undertakings of shape and nerve.

There is pulse and impulse. Clocks in the hall, on kitchen walls and bedside tables.
Verandah swings. Patterns of denial and defeat. Sundials. Shadow.
Open windows. Burls.

There is desire. Lingering desire. Lingering. White trillium and fern.
Dry heat in the poplars. Solitude.

There are voices in the wind. Small stone bowls filled with water
underneath the dripping tap. Bird nests. Clay.

There is turning: to the moon, to myth, to undertone. To the last sentence,
supper, straw. To the finest blade of meaning between what is said and what is not.

There is music. Phrase to phrase, singing to singing. *Dolce. Cantabile.*
Children on their knees. Knuckles. Fingers. Cycles of a life.

There is mourning. Sleep. The small of the back. Held breath.

Breath.

Muse

She comes out of the winter quietly,
a shell of whiteness on her back.
She comes with nothing in her hands.

Which is not to say
she carries nothing.
There is a kind of light
undefined,
a kind of density
that makes me think of water
pooling in the fields
in spring.

She comes as morning comes,
the first sense
almost imagined,
almost real.

Better Days

There are shadows everywhere.
We look left and right
as if one step might be an end,
the last honest move.
Mail trucks roll on, buses,
hot dog vendors talk of better days,
the violinist on the sidewalk packs his case
and heads for home.
And we stand here, dark, dishevelled,
caught between a kind of grace and the underground,
fixed by the fine lyric strain that catches and fades
and catches. This loose, gaunt world.
We are lost to it.
Around the corner: streamers, kites,
the street's become a carnival.
Young men at the bus stop
turn their beautiful heads.

The Rooster

Even through fog
and the leaf-mould haze,
his call alerts us to the fenceline,
the apple tree all limb and lichen,
the climbing roses lapsed.
Winter moss has covered up the patio.
Still, he trumpets his perimeters in the rain,
a featherweight evangelist
gawking and dipping in stride,
ogling the hens, the little garden lamps
along the path, the bench,
the bush, the wily cat.

Townline

The thing is this: there were low clouds
blooming white along the top sides,
down the Townline Creek, fronds of sumac, browned,
and rushes on the bank thinned out to almost nothing.
There were crabapple trees to the left of me,
deep snow, an empty field past that, and up ahead
a tractor idling on the road.
Two figures stood there, maybe three,
farmers in the winter months
who'd say, *too cold*.
Too cold, they'd say and talk about the wind machines,
how many nights they'd turned them on,
who could sleep with the noise,
who couldn't. *There'll be frost damage,
wait and see,* they'd say,
and answer, *sure as anything*.
And they'd watch me come down Townline Road
in slow time, a minute hand before the hour.
I'd see them standing there,
just two of them, not three,
the third a dog,
and then I'd pass the Lambert place,
their voices at my back
like the ends of branches
where the tips, unpruned,
lift slightly into air.

A Gull Will Almost Land

Go on. Everything is good.
Up ahead a gull will almost land in front of you,
its wings will catch the current on a knife-edge,
its flimsy element of bone
will keep it motionless above the ground
for just so long,
and that pure pose will meet the light
as if a god had ordered it
to catch your eye. Go on.
We are all defined by something like surrender,
not a giving in exactly,
not a yielding,
but suspension, perfect justice
as the holding becomes opening,
as the moment of arrival on dry ground,
small and blazing with intent,
becomes departure.

Pianists at Night

At midnight we walked with the music
still burning our fingers.
We knew it that way. On the skin.
Snow fell in the winter months.
Sometimes the cold left a seal on our foreheads
reminding us: the world still lives,
still eats, still takes the garbage out
and sleeps with its face to the wall.
Sometimes a certain phrase
would stay longer than the others.
We'd play it on imaginary keys in our pockets,
as if our fingers were mouths
and singing. Street lights
made perfect circles up the avenue.

Dust and Salt

What have I ever done
but breathe into the wind moving
past me, carrying my breath
with dust and salt into oblivion.
I've slept through years.
If in the moment of dry things
I have wondered
and turned,
no one's known.
I may have spoken in the night
once or twice. I may have suffered.
And the band of sky,
enormous overhead –
what have I to do with that?
Nothing, say the crowds
that shelter here with me.
Nothing at all.

Passing By

I saw your face,
your head and shoulders turn toward me
in a camera's click as I drove by.
We never spoke.
But your hair is dark, I know.
You hadn't shaved
and in your look I saw a fierceness
and a flicker of, what was it, claim? Denial?
Fear? It wasn't anything to do with me.
I wondered if you might be a new father,
a new student or new lover. Did you sleep the night before?
Were you angry at a friend? All of it irrelevant.
You were hurrying to cross before the changing light.
Past the hill, the university,
the bay was perfectly blue
and I was thinking of my son,
knowing I'd remember your concentrated look and this,
this would be more than the chance, more than the second
it took, more than the brilliance of sea water
past the edge of your shape
and the white road going on down.

La cathédrale engloutie

A haze hangs over the streets,
an impression of light.
But there's a magnificent pull
in the way its being here is also
its abandoning.
Of us. Our small lives.
This may have been what Debussy imagined,
a cathedral rising from the water.
Streaming bells and weight,
columns of sound
becoming shimmer, octave ballast
working up to transformation
and then distance, filigree.
We may have had a sense of this
in the Place Dauphin
as we sat under the plane trees in late afternoon,
the leaves slowly falling on us.
So early, we marvelled, in July.
Or was it not late afternoon but evening?
Were the cafes almost closing?
Except for the leaves,
nothing was moving.
Pianissimo.
Above the lawn, circles of flies,
almost transparent, pelt themselves
into the static air.

Open Bloom

Finally
you're driving into inhalation, fields
crazy green, the borders rolled out and flaunting it.
And into something like redemption too,
from your watchman's duties, the hours of waiting
in shadow and grime for the pitch of something absolute,
the long held note at the end of everything,
a deft, whispered charge: leave now.
Take nothing with you but the image,
scent, the unbreaking line.

II

After

After she was gone
and the house emptied of her books and calendars,
her pots, the tins and vegetables,
after the combs had been gathered from her dresser drawers
and the sweater hanging on the back of her chair
was taken off by someone as a gift or keepsake
and the chair pushed in,
I went into her room.
I lay down on her bed
and felt the shape of her.
The maple leaves were shaking in the yard,
the sky a clear, steel blue. July.
Only weeks between her thoughts
and mine, there on the bed,
the window open and the maple tree.
And I remembered
how she always thought of summer sadly
as the slow beginning of less light.

Getting the Chimney Repaired

The man from Holland stands beside the scaffold
saying, oh, it breaks my heart.
I taught him everything I could, how to play chess,
ride a bicycle, how to swim, and after,
how to roll the towel and dry his back,
you know, the shimmy. Now I only see my grandson
twice a year. It breaks my heart.
And then we talk of war, of Amsterdam, the bombing
in the cities. We talk of how my mother made it out,
how her people worked to get ahead, how I must know
all about it: refugees, displacement, fear,
how cold the winters were.
I must have heard, he says. I did.
I sat at the old brown table, listening,
words like openings, liked cracked boards and walls
and northern trains and children's hands
with nothing in them at the windows.
Words like holes.
The storytellers just a little older than this man,
who takes another load of bricks up the scaffold
to the chimney where he fits them
side by side and spreads the mortar over them
to last, he says, as long as I live
and longer still. After that, he says,
who knows?

Third Floor, Queenston Street Wing

The men are old and almost naked in the ward.
They lie with their arms and legs splayed out
as if to say, look at us. Look at our bodies.
Like clothes hanging out to dry.
The wind taunts us, dogs play at our heels,
the sun chafes and burns but we feel no shame.
Imagine us coming up the old farm banks and trails,
the gully bush. Imagine the sumac and spruce,
the shades of berries and hips. Imagine us young and laughing,
leaning into higher ground, wild with the climb.
If there's a shadow of grit in the line of our jaws
as we lie here now, if you see
hardness or flint, even fear,
imagine our greed.

Tulips

I was not prepared.
The clock on the wall marked the time
like a tiny hammer tapping wood.
The windows were still closed.
It could have been a Sunday afternoon of childhood,
white tablecloths, roast beef at lunch, a nap.

But the quiet was a different kind of quiet.
As if a voice could speak but wouldn't.
As if silence could be moveable, a heavy dresser
or commode, but obstinate.
Outside the yard was a lagoon of rain,
the hedge a dark, dripping wall.

And so the orange was dazzling.
An armful of tulips in the old green jar
opened in the middle of the room,
assuming light.

At First

At first I wanted anonymity,
to be lost in concrete halls and elevators,
markets and cathedrals, city squares.
I wanted music on buses and trains to change me
and tell no one. I wanted to be poor.
But shadows fell and lifted,
a few good measures bloomed.
The stone-white tone that held its pitch
beyond the traffic noise and barking dogs,
the keys rattling in the locks,
began to fade.
Skaters circled the bandshell in the park
early in the afternoons.
There were choirs sometimes,
sometimes a thin resonance.
Gorgeous broken lines of light
slashed the outskirts of the city.

Stamina

To outlast dawn,
the calamity of noon.
Vines trailing from the eaves,
the porch enclosed.
Late afternoon: to lie completely still
and wait for what you love.
Have you known this?
And the night then,
have you known its double life?
The tenderness and failing
coming down at once.

William Street Elegies

Openings in Trees

We see them at the table pouring tea
or bending down among the roses.
Their tall shadows pass along the sidewalks of a town
and through the openings in trees.
Sometimes we hear their voices in the evening,
sometimes in dreams or when we read.
We hear them as a conscience: soft, insistent,
as if air were medium enough.
They never ask us to remember,
only leave their doors unlocked at night
expecting us, a lamp left on.
And we imagine winters without solace,
we imagine loss, repentance, mercy.
Love: we wonder at the old poverty,
the heavy stoop. Still they watch us
with the tired, clear eyes of chess players
who have thought out every move behind them,
every move ahead and lost.
Want less, they say,
or nothing.

for L

Sometimes an old woman sings to me,
the snow outside, the white of it,
reflected on her face.
Sometimes she looks past me,
past the winter and the whiteness into long time,
as long as a river of ice that turns and turns
through the valleys of dark pine and moss
to a northern sea.
Her arms rest on the arms of the chair
and she sighs with the river,
the length of it, with the rocks
that line the shores
like voices left to harden there.

for P

I knew nothing of transcendence then,
but the willow was something
and the way the garden narrowed past the shed.
Even now I have the shapes of things
but not the whole, its space and volume,
the undertow.
Solid walls I have, vegetable rows,
a sun porch never used,

a chair, white pail, a hedge,
but not the shadow
spreading over fields and borders,
plains and checkpoints,
rows of closing doors and trains
running through a sweep of steppes.
I have only the rim
where it begins to open into darkness.

for S

Where are the thoughtful ones
who brought out cake and coffee in the afternoons,
gooseberries there in the garden among the currants,
sun on the windowsills.
Where is the violin heard through the door
and the ironing board against the wall,
the small boxes of thread and spools,
and letters held with paper clips.
And where are the words not written there,
the other words
that stayed in the air of thin pines
and arctic grief,
the low stars.

for F

There was no more exile, no more sanctity
or silence or more love
than there was. And no less.
It was the old man standing in the evening
in his Sunday shirt, the sleeves rolled up,
the tip of his cigarette a firefly above the lawn.
It was the dark cover of mulberries in July
and the purple mouths of children in the shadows there.
It was the ashtray on the arm of the chair,
books lining the stairs, tapping rain,
the smell of soup in the kitchen
and black bread and nothing more.
What exists existed there.
The spirit floundering and being saved
again and again in the ordinary hours.
The fountain in the garden like a simple well,
the poplars, past the hedge,
the *sommerhaus* with its green roof.

Yellow Chair

At last the fidelity of things opens our eyes.
Zbigniew Herbert – "Stool"

The yellow chair is loyal, there's no doubt
about its steadfast heart,
lifted from the hardiest wood.
How else could we sit here day after day,
shifting our weight from leg to leg?

At the Bus Stop

He brushes her hair aside
and brings the camera in so close
it almost touches her skin.
He tries to get at what he thinks is essence,
the pure form of her, the cell.
But so much rides on curve and line,
swell and shade, the possible arc –
he hasn't thought about deep focus yet
or span – he settles on one retina,
the corner of a tooth, one lobe.

Eva

Maybe she knew what she was doing
following him to the bunker
like she did.
Maybe the girl who hung from fence posts
making faces for the camera,
who water-skied and danced,
who took pleasure in hats
and swimming and shoes,
wasn't as simple
as they thought.
Maybe she knew
the way we know sometimes.
Enormities.
A solid wall comes down,
quietly, intact,
locking into place something not yet said,
not even thought,
but heard.
That low whirring in the inner ear,
the wolf ear,
barely turned.

Soup

In the camps, he said,
the bowl of soup
is everything.
It's all you think about.
Soup is thought.
And he looked at the curtain
moving slightly
where she'd left the window open
for the roses.

To Adam Zagajewski

I read your poems and remember two old people
in their quiet house on William Street,
next to two more people in their quiet house
and two or three more down the street
and on the other streets and others still.
No one spoke on Sunday afternoons
as the sun warmed the tables and books
and coffee steamed in little cups,
but as night came
with its shadows and sighs,
the walls moved in like long-dead friends
and fathers, sisters, sons,
and there were careful words
said as if the saying were another kind of loss,
as if words could be the ashes of a heart, windblown.
Afterward, another pot of coffee went around,
the old people prayed and waved to us
going out the door and to the car, the others
from the other houses leaving too,
all of us driving into the soft rain
of our new lives.

Sotto Voce

It has more to do with vowels,
I think, or with the cello
played in an empty room
at night.
That small voluptuousness.
A bloom of hesitation.
Is it modesty? Or loss?
Could it be the squint of listening?
Or possibly,
and maybe this is getting close,
the undervoice,
barely opening its dark throat.

The Hired Man

A rifle in his hand, disgruntled,
dark with nerve, he crossed
the packing yard to where my father stood.

From high up in the barn
I saw his black head lurch,
a flash of gun, my father

springing into endless time.
I heard the metal snap, the cartridges
kicked out and angry steps
across the gravel lot.

Down below the work went on,
the packers silent at the belt,
but in the loft the dust rang bullet fire,
the roof blew open over me
and swallows shot through
crazy with light.

Cicadas

He said what I was hearing
was the sound of hydro wires, a buzzing sound
that still reminds me of those dry-mouth days of August,
days of dust and diesel fuel, hot peaches in our hands,
the high noon of summer beating the orchards white.
It still reminds me of our shorts worn thin as the weeds that grew
waist high in the ditches, our scabbed-up knees below the hems
coming down, and the road we walked along,
my brother and I, popping tar bubbles under our shoes.
I can't see his face as it was then,
as if I never looked at him – I did – it wasn't that
but a knowing he was there that I remember,
a second me or more of me, a longer arm or leg, a third hand,
fourth, the way we know as children
sameness, taking everything as fixed and right and infinite.
And so we walked under those black wires
sizzling through the pears past Fraser's place and toward the lake,
listening to that sound so like the one cicadas make, believing in it
as a certainty, as we believed in God, in leather belts,
in the deep pit of the well and the one square of light
high in the barn, where the dust moved with the swallows
that lit the space like dark, shooting stars.
The restlessness, the wonder, walking
side by side, not knowing insect life

could rattle in our ears like that, not knowing much at all
but that we were thirsty, that the sky was a smooth dome
over our heads, and the tracing of the city barely visible
across the lake was only that, an outline of the world.
The ditches overgrown with chicory and Queen Anne's lace
were what mattered in the moment
and the moment mattered on and on
and on. I know now
the sound cicadas make.
I know that we were wrong.
The sudden flare of listening
is itself a kind of pitch. I know
what stays in the ear is closer to song
than speech, and echo is one turn
from silence, one turn
from never having heard at all.

Violets

And so we live with calamity every day,
its enormous shadow tailing us,
always pushing in and draining light.
We walk to the end of the block
and see it standing there, kitty-corner
to the bank or out behind the parking lot.
We come in off the back step
and feel a breath of something half-familiar,
bold, as we close the door behind us,
make the tea. We get used to it.
Like the bungalow standing next to the high-rise.
Violets grow in the window shamelessly.
The young couple sit at the kitchen table
eating toast in the morning shadow
just the same.

III

Premonition

Still: brown wrens sifting up and out
from the undergrowth,
colliding plates beneath the surface, heat.
Still: steep hills, acacia, phlox,
the drought of white stone walls
and poplar drift.

And we will not be here.
Not one of us. The wind will move
in the trees that have outlived us.
There will be other clearings,
silences, other breaths.
There will be a deep disowning
and we will be the past,
a rock face in the mist
above the beaches
where the tide comes in
and pulls away.

What I Was Told to Do with My Soul

Leave it in the hands of someone who knows best
what to do with its dark folds and mystery,
someone who can see its possibilities
without bias, even from a distance,
and shape it into something leaner
with a purpose, who can take it from you easily
as if it were a simple loaf of bread you'd offered
or a song.
Let it go.
And lightly then, lightly
as the poplars in the churchyard used to catch the wind
that flipped the leaves like silver pages
(you would hear the whirl before you turned around to see it),
like that, let it be taken.
And if you feel a weightlessness where you remember pull,
you can fill the space with work or silence
and if that's not enough,
the calls of killdeer split the air at dawn.
You've listened in the dead of rising
in the lonely days. You've heard them in your sleep.
Crickets under the thick leaves of cabbage
blow the nights to smithereens. You understand.
There will always be wind and dropping skies
and the search for what is sure: bark,
dirt, an apple from the bushel in late fall,
a hard hand, brokenness.

You'll carry something in its place,
the thin red line of morning, for example,
coming toward you like a word
you spoke before you spoke in words,
like a stone you carried once and threw away.

Temptation

It was already dark
at one of those roadside inns
when he said, tell me,
he said, tell me everything about you.
I want to know it all.
And she was flattered, really.
But maybe not enough.
She thought about the risk in knowledge,
Eve, the fall,
the serpent's place within the world,
and trees and shining ferns and bougainvillea
the colour of wine or lapis lazuli
and said, too softly,
can we order now?

November

The city is pummelled now.
Nothing can ever be lifted.
Smoke, the smell of pine and yellow plum
hang on the branches
as the light lowers itself to its knees.

Children run from school with empty coat sleeves
flapping like loose wings behind them.
Only their faces are clear.
Homeless men walk along the boulevard
searching for some elemental shift

and I wait for a solid language,
more particulate, more finely scored and staved.
Reconsider weight, I tell myself,
this beautiful plunge.

Suite for Tools

Hoe

Lean as the thin-lipped aunt that snips
loose threads with her teeth,
but smooth handled from long use
and warm in the hand.
A row of workers in the field
swing in unison, hats
like halos in the milky heat.

Shovel

Never called a spade,
it stayed in the realm of muck and sweat.
But the swing of it could take you away,
a downbeat and slur, drop and heave
in one kinetic phrase.

Ladder

My father handled a ladder easily,
set it firm against a sturdy branch
and clambered up as if he'd never stop,
the top rung nothing to consider
on his way to open sky,
the fruit tree incidental.

Plow

The extravagant musk we remember.
Black ground worked up in spring, all loam
and vowel: a deeper language
holding us to strange, invisible systems
of place. Dark matter turned
to the understorey light.

Wheelbarrow

Perfect for hauling children or dirt,
but one wheel,
as someone realized long ago,
is never enough for easy travel.
And so it goes the way it goes.
Lumbering.
For her birthday once
my mother got a yellow one.

Harness

Someone always started singing in the trees.
Early. Someone in a harness.
All the weight of the basket under the ribs.
But free arms, nimble fingers,
a voice able still
to improvise.

Devotion

The eye catches the furthest ridge of land,
holds the arc and solder of it like a welding rod,
nothing but flame, forge, a metal line.
Nothing but the mid-eye force.
It hammers its knowing into the place,
its being into the resonant light,
its dying into the form.

The Crow

Keep your eye on it,
high in the branches of the fir,
setting its small, black back against a wind
that slags hard off the beaches of Margaret Bay.
It lives on the tang of cold, the cloudlessness,
without intent.
It is everything and nothing
as the wind is more than force and less,
as you are watching and not watching,
waiting and not waiting.
Imagine a time after its flight: the branch bare
but the spirit of its shape stamped there
as long as you remember that ruffled back
in the metal-gray sky, as long as you see it,
in absence, more clearly.

In the Waiting Room

The man who walks out into the day and the city
isn't you, but there is something in his shoulders,
in the way he holds his back
as if he's lived with reticence and dream
too many years, that reminds me
of your slenderness,
and I wonder, sitting here,
if someone ever watched you walk
from shadow into light, years ago,
someone seeing someone else in you,
remembering.
And isn't this the finest bloom of loss?
The opening of recognition into all its other lives.
In an instant: resonance
reminding us of everything at once
and love.

Sisters

They hung the deer by their hooves from the rafters.
Seven deer, as many men,
and they left them there all night,
dark shapes in the barn, the deer spirits hovering.
In the morning they came to tear down the hides.
Each man took a side and pulled from the cut
with the sound of a tree cracked loose
in lightning, split like that,
the bodies swaying purple from the hooks.
We stood there, you and I, taking it in,
storing an enormous forming burl.
Wild grains we couldn't name. Swirls.
Something about nakedness and force,
shame and pity, wilderness and men
and work and certainty.
Something about lost skins piled on the floor
in the early light
that I remember shone
on your small round head.

Underground

The absence of light in these underground rooms
has left me thin as a stalk in winter.
I lean toward what I believe is a brightening,
some thin blue beam that would show me words
others have left on the flowstones.
My fingers trace the braille that rises and falls.
Behind me in this particular dark comes
the pressure of what can only be called wind,
pushing me further into the night
that is not night.

The Nail

Up on the roof the nail went through his knee
but the others were sure: no bone, they said,
it only hit the meat.
An ambulance came and took him away
and the three that were left
looked at the place where he'd been lying
as if he'd stayed there
but folded in and small.
I saw it go in, said the first.
I feel like doing nothing, said the second,
and the third looked down
and said it had happened to him once too.
A nail like that. The same.
They drank the coffee I gave them
and went back to the roof shaking their heads
as if they'd looked too hard at the sun,
too long, and a pin of fire had left a whiteness
where it should have been clear.

To Walk into That Beauty

To walk into that beauty
the way he walks into the barn.
Long limbs of light and purpose. Lankiness.
And something else: as if it costs him.
As if to ride the arm of heat
coming from the burnt-out fields
is a matter of fidelity.
Only that.
To enter raw and squinting,
measuring the dark,
knowing where everything is.

The Polish Class Sits Down to Dinner

This table isn't long enough
to hold our consonantal efforts,
or wide enough to wrestle seven cases,
herd in the palatals, the plural forms of verbs,
the *pan* or *pani,* or the nasal vowels.
But the candles in small glasses end to end,
flicker optimistically, the dogs
heavy at our feet
are nonchalant
(they've dealt with verbal inconsistencies before),
and now the dusk just moving in behind our chairs
becomes the perfect present tense.
We shine.
Tamara, bring out the bowls and platters,
the steaming sausages and wine,
the bigos and bread, the poppyseed cakes.
We understand this middle distance.
We've raised the white flags of our senses,
declared ourselves beguiled.
To Chopin mazurkas,
to Mickiewicz and Milosz
we raise our glasses.
On our lips a hint of cinnamon, pear,
elderberry and sage.
Something like dialect is taking us in,
something like speaking in tongues.

Metaphor

The willows go down creaking on their knees.
Pond grasses lean into noon, blonde
with animal warmth: wild dogs, jays and quail.
Dark pitches of night air move among the vines and lilies
even in the day. The frogs are booming.

I tell you there's a crevice wide enough
to matter here. More than words.
Stones fall over the edge into the darkness,
rivulets of water, bits of earth and root.
You can estimate the depth by the small,
struck sound from the bottom,
how an echo rises to the surface,
but with greater clarity,
greater force.

Restraint

These cherries
picked before the sun
scalded the tractor hood
and scorched the barn door handles
making them too hot to touch,
were carried into the laneway by the Polish women,
still in shoulder harnesses, who eat their bread and cheese
under the trees, on cannery crates,
in kerchiefs the colour of geraniums
and summer tablecloths.
Mrs. Kanya takes her shirt off in the heat
to fan herself, while the northern men,
down from the reserves,
turn their faces to the blue lake
out of gentleness,
and the Italian women who speak a language of vowels
and wrap their sandwiches in scarves,
laugh from under the shed roof, one
showing her gold tooth like a flash of thigh,
the other only grateful.
And the men from Jamaica
dream in deep shade
after their singing
as they knocked the stone-hard peaches
from the branches with their thinning sticks,
made the light-haired girl listening
from the back end of the pickup,
eating watermelon pickles,
feel like dancing.

Now

> *Now all the darkness is in the leaves...*
> Margaret Avison – "Twilight"

I hear my children's voices in the room around me now.
Treble voices rising with the day.
The light from the windows is steep white,
as if holiness were a simple matter of curtains and filtered sun
on a mid-week morning.
A rooster cracks the distance.
Transparency: is this what draws us back?
Was it the white sheets hanging on the line in a wind from the lake,
my mother's long brown arms working with the clothespins
she kept in a wooden basket on the grass?
Was it her low whistling?
Was it the piles of laundry here on the floor
and my own sons rolling, rolling
in the deep cottons, their backs and shoulders,
knees, as round as their mouths and the circle of desire
that made them in the nights
those early days?
We can never leave.
When we ran along the packed-down dirt of orchard lanes,
between the rows of plum and pear and the sun
burned a circle on our foreheads
like a mark of grace,
whatever it was in the flight of the red-tailed hawk,

whatever was there in the brightness,
stayed. We know it by the light
from here to there
and here.
My children, run.
Your faces stay with me,
now all the darkness is in the leaves.

Wonder

It was the tenderness: a door left open
to the light from the hall like an outstretched hand,
a last look back at an empty kitchen chair
turned to the window and the world,
cups carried to the table in pairs,
hands on the keys, wrong notes
played quietly. It was the spirit giving in
and giving out, saying, I cannot do more,
see more, live more.
But it was never resignation,
only wonder at the cost.

Winter

The snow has stopped falling now.
A bell of white encloses me.
I breathe in the taste of water
as if breath has more to do with memory,
relinquishing.
I don't hear it now.
The music. As if breath
has more to do with silence.

Acknowledgements

I am deeply grateful to Sue Sinclair for her editorial insight and grace. Many thanks also to Nick Thran for his deft copy-editing, and to Cheryl Dipede for her artistry. To Kitty Lewis, my hearty appreciation for so much behind-the-scenes support.

A very special thank you to Jan Zwicky.

To the Canada Council for the Arts for its support, and to the editors of *The Malahat Review*, *The Fiddlehead*, *The New Quarterly*, and *The Antigonish Review*, who published earlier versions of some of these poems, my sincere appreciation.

To Amalie Enns and Diane Enns, heartfelt gratitude for literary and familial support, and to my sons, Francis, Elliot, and Lawren Rowe, warm, warm thanks for both inspiration and distraction.

KAREN ENNS worked as a classical pianist for almost twenty years before publishing her first book of poetry. *That Other Beauty* was nominated for the Gerald Lampert Award. A native of southern Ontario, where she grew up in a Mennonite farming community, she lives in Victoria, BC.